YOGA

THE SCIENCE OF SELF REALIZATION

GW00480896

Other Books By The Author

Kundalini The Energy Of Awakening
Ascension The Path To Liberation
Unity The Evolution Of Consciousness
Lightbearer
Dark Knight Of The Soul
Heartbeat Of The Earthmother

All books available at:
justinwesenberg.com

YOGA

THE SCIENCE OF SELF REALIZATION

JUSTIN WESENBERG

This book is dedicated
To the light in your soul
Through the practice of yoga
You become whole

TABLE OF
CONTENTS

KNOW THYSELF

Jnana: The Yoga Of Knowledge   15
The Missing Piece   19
Lemuria   25
Cosmic Flow   29
Kundalini Rising   33
Jewel Of The Earth   37
Deep Divers   41
Shiva Linga   45
The River   51
Yellow Galactic Warrior   55
Universal Force   61
Galactic Gateway   65

LOVE THYSELF

Bhakti: The Yoga Of Love   71
The Mother   75
Lands Unknown   81
Heart Teacher   87
Inner Space   93
Sadasiva   97
Grim Reaper   101
Spring Showers   105
Guruji   109
Hidden Currents   113
World Of The Ancients   117
Guardian Angel   121

SERVE THYSELF

Karma: The Yoga Of Action   129

Divine Light   133

Lakshmi   139

Quantum Leap   145

Yogananda   149

The Light   155

Omnipotent   161

Moksha   165

Inner Eye   169

White Crystal Wizard   173

Ganesha   179

Osiris   183

About The Author   189

The Invitation   191

KNOW THYSELF

JNANA: THE YOGA OF KNOWLEDGE

In the Bhagavad Gita Krishna outlines to Arjuna the three paths of yoga that one can follow in order to find Moksha, spiritual freedom. These paths are jnana yoga, the yoga of knowledge, bhakti yoga, the yoga of love, and karma yoga, the yoga of action.

In jnana yoga the yogi is focused on attaining knowledge of the divine through self reflection, study of the scriptures, and being immersed in nature.

All three paths are used to help people reach the divine through the methods that are most appropriate for them. The path of knowledge is most relevant to people who have an inclination towards intellectual pursuits and logic.

What does it take
To feel fulfilled
You will find inner peace
When your mind is stilled

This does not mean that only one path can be followed though. For the quickest results it is recommended that the yogi follows all paths simultaneously.

Swami Sivananda recommends this in his book *The Yoga Of Synthesis*. All paths compliment each other, but some may resonate more strongly than others based on a person's individual preferences.

Jnana, the path of knowledge has been considered the most challenging path to follow as it deals mostly in abstract terms and philosophical questions. If you want to explore this path more deeply ask yourself the question "How can I realize my highest potential as a divine being?"

You will learn to feel
Whole and complete
When you bow in surrender
In a meditative seat

THE MISSING PIECE

From the moment I met you
I could feel it in my soul
You were the missing piece
The one to make me whole

I prayed for you
Under the light of the moon
And when you came into my life
I couldn't help but swoon

No words can describe
How much I cared
But no matter what I did
You were never there

I tried and I tried
I gave and I gave
And at the end of the day
I just felt like a slave

Relationships are
A two way street
And pleasing you
Was no easy feat

THE MISSING PIECE

I was willing to put
My own life aside
To put in the effort
And let go of my pride

Sweeping the problems
Under the rug
All I wanted
Was a nice big hug

To feel close to you
And emotionally connected
But all I felt
Was let down and rejected

I should have been clear
With what I wanted from the start
I had no idea
This would break my heart

I can't deny
The feelings I feel
The pain inside
Just caused me to reel

It's been months now
And I'm still letting go
I'm grateful for this experience
As it's helped me to grow

So that I can release
The things holding me back
Codependency in relationships
And my sense of lack

It's time for me to rise
And lift myself up
And know that I'm responsible
For filling my own cup

So that I can find
The value of my worth
Create with beauty
And start helping the Earth

All I wanted
Was to feel your love
Now I just pray
To the heavens above

THE MISSING PIECE

And ask the angels
To help set me free
So that I can step forward
And be all I can be

It's not easy
Walking forward on your own
But without this experience
I would never have been shown

How to let go
Of the need to please
When I listen to my own heart
Life moves with ease

I'm still looking for someone
Who will really care
So that we can come together
And create a life we can share

I know when I find her
Our hearts will align
And together we will radiate
The light of the divine

LEMURIA

How can we live our life
In eternal peace
When will we allow
The violence to cease

So that we can find
Purity and love
The grace of the divine
The light from above

We all have
Our own path to walk
Where will you be
When death starts to knock

This journey is here
For you to live
Find the love in your heart
And learn to give

This is the highest teaching
The Lemurians share
Unconditional love
Is found in prayer

Let go
Of the need to control
Surrender to the divine
And you become whole

By letting go
Of the need to force
You allow nature
To take its course

Flowing like a river
Down to the ocean
Detach from your thoughts
Let go of the commotion

Then you will exist
In the present state
Where you can stop the violence
And end the hate

Changing the things
You tell yourself
So that you can discover
The greatest wealth

Is not found
In the money in the banks
Bow your head
And learn to give thanks

For the beautiful experience
That life can be
When you practice gratitude
You become free

COSMIC FLOW

Learn to walk the path
That is yours to tread
Life is short
One day you'll be dead

Does that thought scare you
Does it cut you to the bone
When will you learn
To put down the phone

This life is precious
A beautiful gift
And it's up to you
To bring the shift

To the way we choose
To live our lives
From a society in agony
To one that thrives

When we constantly consume
With mindless greed
We begin to lose focus
On what we need

The real values
That make life worth living
Like love, truth
Caring and giving

It is time to rise
And let ourselves shine
So that we can radiate
The light of the divine

Getting lost
In the cosmic flow
Stop trying to control
Learn to let go

You will be shown
What you need to see
So that you can grow
And set other free

From the false belief
That you are not enough
You don't need to fill the void
By buying more stuff

Within you you carry
The golden flame
That will ignite
When you recite my name

Practice the mantra
That was given to you
Within it you'll find
A love that is true

Guiding you along
The path you tread
Dispelling the fear
That one day you'll be dead

By helping you witness
The enlightened state
So that you can learn
To change your fate

KUNDALINI RISING

How can I let go
And release the past
Free myself from these demons
Find peace at last

From the anger and suffering
The fear and doubt
The twisting knots
That make me scream and shout

The emotions are the guides
Of the subconscious mind
When we learn to transmute them
We will no longer be blind

To the way our perspective
Distorts our view
When we learn to observe
We will find what is true

Instead of assuming
Our ego knows best
We can learn to surrender
So that we can be blessed

By willingly admitting
That we do not know
We create the space
To learn and grow

To help us evolve
To start something new
So that love can radiate
In all that we do

You need to have
The courage to rise
When you can't see beyond
The tears in your eyes

These tests that you face
Are the journey of the soul
Teaching you
What it means to be whole

Only by overcoming
The darkness we face
Can we learn to stand
And create new space

Let go of the baggage
Weighing you down
The serpent will rise
And illuminate the crown

Helping you reach
The primordial state
Dissolving your karma
And clearing your slate

So that you can show others
What it means to be free
Illuminate the planet
And help us see

How we can let go
Of the suffering we face
Find peace in our hearts
And transform with grace

JEWEL OF THE EARTH

What if you had
A jewel from the earth
That could show you the truth
What life is worth

To transform your being
Through the purity of light
To cast out the shadows
That creep through the night

Requires you to have
Faith and trust
To fulfill your duty
You do what you must

We all have
Our own calling to follow
If you're off the path
It'll cause you to wallow

Wondering how you got
Stuck in the reeds
While ignoring
All your own needs

JEWEL OF THE EARTH

Start to focus
On self love and self care
Just know that when you pray
The angels are there

Helping you fulfill
Your every need
So that you can serve
And let go of greed

The energy of money
Flows freely through you
When you trust that God
Supports all that you do

To make the world
A beautiful place
So that you can rise
With a smile on your face

Sharing with others
The beauty and wealth
That comes from knowing
The truth of the Self

The jewel is found
In the lotus inside
Trust in your soul
Allow it to guide

Then you will follow
The path that is yours
No longer will your duties
Feel like chores

For you will sense
God all around
Through the ambient air waves
The vibrations of sound

Trust that change
Is right for you
And let love flow
In all that you do

DEEP DIVERS

Why does it feel
Like I am never enough
Why does it always
Have to be so rough

What will it take
To allow me to breathe
When on the inside
My stomach wants to heave

Feeling crippled by anxiety
Fear and dread
Sometimes I wonder
If I'd be better off dead

Life can be hard
When you're finding your path
Spend time with your friends
Let yourself laugh

This is the medicine
That will change your view
So that you can find peace
In all that you do

It triggers chemicals
In our brains
That help us let go
Of the grip on these chains

That keep us trapped
In the fears of the mind
By pinning us down
And making us blind

To the world of abundance
That lies all around
When you need a reminder
Find the plants in the ground

They always have
What they need to live
When we find this in ourselves
We learn to give

For it is in sharing
That we create community
An abundant ecosystem
With new opportunity

You have your gifts
They have been given to you
Share them with others
And love what you do

You always have the power
To choose where you go
Follow your heart
You will learn and grow

And help us create
A world where we can thrive
You'll shout from the rooftops
It feels so good to be alive

Diving deep
To the root of the soul
When you find your center
You become whole

SHIVA LINGA

We pour the water
Over the holy form
We pray to the Guru
Help us weather the storm

The constant battle
That rages inside
Teach us to surrender
And let the light guide

Show us the way
Out of the dark
So that we can see
When we're missing the mark

Straying too far
From the path we have chosen
Letting fear keep us
Paralyzed and frozen

How can we dissolve
Our bondage to this world
So that we can witness
The mystery unfurled

And know the truth
Of how we came to be
Shine your divine light
So that we can see

How we can cross the oceans
Into sacred lands
The power to change
Lies in our hands

It is only through action
That we can change our course
And discover the light
Of the Eternal Source

Guiding us through
Our journey on Earth
So that we can bring about
A planetary rebirth

The consciousness of Oneness
Permeates through us all
It is time to rise
And learn to stand tall

Shine your light
For all the ships out at sea
And you will show them
What it means to be

A heavenly guide
Sent from above
To teach humanity
About the path of love

You will attract
All the abundance and wealth
That comes from understanding
The truth of the Self

You are an unlimited being
Of love and light
Here to guide others
Through the dark of night

They cannot see
Beyond the maya of illusion
This is why they stumble
Lost in confusion

Losing the path
Being led astray
Is it any wonder
That we have lost the way

We need a lighthouse
To guide us through
To cut through the fog
And show us what is true

You came here
Eternal and free
To help guide others
So that they can see

The true goals
The spiritual aims
So they can let go
Of these tiring games

Racing around
Caught in the trap of mind
Is it any wonder
That we seem so blind

To the love that lies
Within us all
We need to listen
And heed the call

The time for change
Has already begun
We step forward together
On the path as One

We bathe the Guru
In his divine form
So we can teach others
How to weather the storm

And let love radiate
In all that we do
So that they can go within
And find what is true

THE RIVER

What will it take
For us to let go
To release our burdens
And get lost in the flow

To surrender all
That we think we know
To empty ourselves
So we have room to grow

We are constantly berated
By the need to consume
We are never enough
Once we leave the womb

Companies will always tell us
What we need
So we can fuel
Their corporate greed

While they rape the planet
And destroy our home
When we leave this place
We do so alone

THE RIVER

We cannot take
Our money and wealth
All that we have
Is what lies in our Self

Infinite and eternal
Expansive and free
When will you allow yourself
To truly see

The radiant light
That lies within you
So that you can stand for truth
In all that you do

You don't need
To sell your soul
Find peace in your heart
Love is the goal

When you learn to cultivate
The inner space
It will change your thoughts
And put a smile on your face

So that you can be free
Like the birds in the sky
Maybe it's time to stop
And ask yourself why

Why are we polluting
And destroying the Earth
When will we learn to recognize
What life is really worth

How can we change
The society in which we live
When will we learn to love
And let ourselves give

So that we can be
All we can be
Find love in our hearts
And set ourselves free

YELLOW GALACTIC WARRIOR

Sing the song
Of the galactic tone
And ensure that no one
Has to walk alone

For in this journey
That we all take
We get to choose
What me make

Of the time that we have
On the material plane
How can we use our actions
To help others gain

A greater understanding
Of who they are
They've gone through the struggle
And come this far

Unconditional love
Is the truth of the soul
Realize your nature
And you become whole

YELLOW GALACTIC WARRIOR

Like the galaxies that spiral
Up overhead
Don't allow yourself to wander
Like the living dead

The truth of your being
Is eternal and free
What will it take
For you to truly see

The radiant light
That lies inside
Surrender your fears
Let go of your pride

It is only through surrender
And letting go
That we create new space
So that we can grow

To become our best selves
To know who we are
Let the ferryman's staff guide you
To the wisdom of the stars

When you see the galaxies
Spiraling overhead
You will come to understand
That it's all in your head

The suffering, the torture
The fear you face
Trust in the light
And rise with grace

For you are here
To help others shine
To teach them the power
Of a love that is divine

Find this love
Within yourself
And you will know
The greatest wealth

Lies deep within
The center of being
It will help you dissolve
The illusion you're seeing

So that you can learn
To find what is true
And stand up for love
In all that you do

UNIVERSAL FORCE

The voice of the universe
The highest guide
Trust in the divine
Let go of your pride

Then you will find
Life moving with ease
As you let go
Like the leaves on the trees

Letting the wind
Carry you down
Only through grace
Can you illuminate the crown

Allowing you to see
Beyond the veil
What would you do
If you could not fail

How would you change
Your inner state
How would you serve
When you control your fate

Sharing with others
Your beautiful gift
As the maya of illusion
Begins to lift

So that they can see
A new reality
That lies beyond
All this brutality

Awaken the world
To the fifth dimension
You will learn to release
Your inner tension

By following the path
That is yours to walk
You focus your gaze
Like the eyes of a hawk

Allowing you to manifest
What you truly need
Learn to share
And let go of greed

Then you will find
Where true wealth lies
When you see the love that sits
Behind another's eyes

Showing you
The light of the soul
Reminding you
What it means to be whole

GALACTIC GATEWAY

Mantras are frequencies
Of a galactic tone
Recited by us
To make the Earth a home

For all beings to live
Open and free
Expand to your true self
Then you will see

How the vibration of love
Can affect real change
When you shift your mindset
And begin to rearrange

The pieces in your life
Where they need to fit
What do you say
When you want to quit

Something you know
Is unhealthy for you
Do you convince yourself
That it's not really true

Have the courage to face
What holds you back
Let go with grace
Your sense of lack

For you are abundant
An infinite being
Expand your perspective
And what you are seeing

When you learn to let go
Of limiting views
Like those on TV
While watching the news

You will understand
The power to create
Is what shapes your life
And changes your fate

You must have the courage
To take action and go
Trust in the divine
Then you will grow

Release the need
To be in control
Then you will know
The truth of the soul

The Eternal Mystery
The everlasting seed
Trust in the divine
Is all you will need

LOVE THYSELF

BHAKTI: THE YOGA OF LOVE

Bhakti is the yoga of love and devotion and is often practiced towards a personal God. The identification to a supreme force could be towards anything and anyone including: Jesus, Buddha, Shiva, Krishna, Mother Earth, the cosmos, or anything else you desire. It is up to you to decide what you choose to love and honour in your life.

The practice of living lovingly flows in all directions regardless of whether or not you believe in a divine source at all. This is why humanity feels so disconnected, we have lost our connection to Source energy. It is the energy of Spirit that supports us and sustains us. It is through love that we find the truth waiting to reveal itself.

When life becomes
Too much to bear
Bring your palms together
Bow in prayer

Love is the root of all spiritual traditions and practices. It is through love that we come to know the truth of the Self. The infinite and eternal light that lies within.

Your very essence is love and at this time in our evolution we are being called to activate the power of unconditional love that lies within us. It is the unifying force that brings us into harmony with ourselves, each other, and the planet. Through the unity of love we will find our highest light.

Bhakti, the path of love is best suited to those who are more emotional in nature. If you want to follow the path of bhakti yoga ask yourself the question "How can I love unconditionally?"

The force that sets
Celestial bodies in motion
Is the same that is found
Through love and devotion

THE MOTHER

Prayer is
The most powerful force
To help you chart
A new course

Weaving you through
The currents of life
So that you can give up
Your inner strife

And trust the journey
That lies ahead
It's up to you
To visualize in your head

The kind of world
That you want to see
It's time to fly
And be all you can be

To help us change
The planet at large
We need you to step up
And learn to take charge

THE MOTHER

Of the powerful force
That lies within you
It can change the face
Of all that you do

Embodying love
With will and devotion
Will help you cut through the noise
And all the commotion

Of how the world
Is going to end
The illusion you see
Is all pretend

Just a story
Made up in your mind
There to make you
Completely blind

To the true nature
That lies in your soul
Discovering this truth
Will make you whole

No longer a slave
To the senses of the body
You will enter
Nirvikalpa Samadhi

A beautiful state
Of glorious bliss
Nothing compares
To the glorious kiss

That we get from the Goddess
The Mother of the Earth
Here to help us
Find our worth

All we must do
Is bow and pray
And ask Her
To show us the way

To find inner peace
And love in yourself
Know that this
Is the greatest wealth

And it can come
When we bow in prayer
And know that The Mother
Is always there

LANDS UNKNOWN

What would you do
If you could not fail
What would it take
To set your sails

To chart the waters
Into lands unknown
To show other the truth
About what you've been shown

The secrets of life
Go to the brave
You didn't come here
To be a slave

To corporate control
And government rule
To follow the masses
Is the path of the fool

You came here
To be free and shine
To teach them the power
Of a love that is divine

Let yourself radiate
Like the sun in the sky
It's time to spread your wings
And let yourself fly

So that others can see
The beauty and wealth
That comes from knowing
The truth of the Self

Eternal and unchanging
Holy and pure
This connection to love
Will make you strong and sure

That the path you are taking
Is the right one for you
Most of us walk forward
Not having a clue

You must know
The values you hold
This life is your journey
Step out of the mold

The body you carry
Is not a one-size-fits-all
You are not here
As another brick in the wall

You came here
Eternal and free
To help others become
All they can be

We need you now
More than you know
To help us learn
Expand and grow

To illuminate the shackles
That hold us back
The thoughts we carry
About our sense of lack

So that we can rise
Like the stars in the sky
Dissolve the past
Let the ego die

And know the truth
That lies in your heart
Step forward with courage
And play your part

HEART TEACHER

Sometimes it feels
Like the sky is painted with gray
When we stumble through life
Feeling like we have lost the way

We go through the motions
We do what we're told
Is this all there is to life
As we begin to grow old

It is only in silence
That your heart will speak
Trust that it will help you
Find what you seek

We all deserve
To feel fulfilled
When you know what you want
It's easier to build

The life of your dreams
What you wish to see
Know that you have the power
To set yourself free

HEART TEACHER

From the shackles and burdens
That hold you back
Your limited mindset
Your sense of lack

Just close your eyes
Breathe in and out
Release your fears
Your sense of doubt

Do not be afraid
Of the power you hold
You are unique
Step out of the mold

Society wants you
To stay on the wheel
Continue the rat race
Numb the way you feel

Is this really
What you came here to do
It's time to search within
And find what is true

You came here to serve
For the highest good of all
Find your courage and strength
Stop playing so small

We need you
And your beautiful light
To illuminate the planet
And help us shine bright

To cast out the shadows
To awaken the Earth
Find your strength inside
And discover your worth

It is only through harnessing
The spiritual force
That we can create a new life
And chart a new course

That aligns us with
The truth in our soul
To feel fulfilled
Is a wonderful goal

Go within
And listen to your guide
Know the truth
That lies inside

Your heart is speaking to you
Let it guide the way
It will dissolve the darkness
The sky of gray

So that you can share
The truth of the light
Like the blazing sun
You will learn to shine bright

INNER SPACE

Thank you God
For this beautiful day
Thank you God
For showing me the way

To help me realize
The gifts of the soul
To connect to your essence
And learn to become whole

Spending time in nature
Under the beautiful sunshine
Helps me to realize
A love that is divine

Infinite and eternal
Like the universe above
How can I learn
To radiate this love

And share this light
With all that I meet
I bow in service
Humbly at your feet

So that I can show others
The beauty of your grace
Change their thoughts
And put a smile on their face

Learning to serve
Will make you divine
By giving to others
You let yourself shine

Sharing with others
What you know is true
Will help you to serve
In the work that you do

You are abundant
Unlimited and free
When you come to know God
Then you will see

The beautiful being
That you truly are
Carved from the light
In the birth of a star

We all come
From the same cosmic source
When we realize this
It will change our course

To live our lives
Enjoying every day
The present is a gift
It will show you the way

To find inner peace
To be happy and whole
To find love in your heart
And truth in your soul

Then you will learn
To share the grace
That comes from cultivating
The inner space

SADASIVA

How can I break
Out of this cage
To free my mind
I start burning the sage

Igniting the bhasma
At your lotus feet
I close my eyes
And let my palms meet

I bow my head
In humility to you
To the guru of guru's
Help me change my view

So that I can release
My grip on the past
Help me end the chatter
Find peace at last

For it is only
By letting go
That we create space
For new seeds to grow

To co-create
With the universal source
It is time we charted
A new course

To a life filled
With love and light
Help us cast out the darkness
So we can shine bright

And teach others
About the truth of the One
Illuminating the planet
Like the blazing sun

Showing them
The truth of the soul
Be your authentic self
Step into your role

We all have
Our own part to play
It's up to you
To do what you say

Don't be afraid
To fall on your face
All warriors rise
With love and grace

It is only through stepping
Out onto the field
That you will find the courage
To share the power you wield

An infinite being
Eternal and divine
You came to the planet
So that you could shine

To stand up for love
With all your might
It is time that you rise
And share the power of the light

GRIM REAPER

Sometimes in life
You just break down and cry
Curl up into a ball
And wish you would die

I know how it feels
To be gripped in fear
Stumbling through life
When the path isn't clear

Constantly feeling
Like you are never enough
Why does life
Have to be so tough

When every day is a struggle
Right until the end
How can we heal these wounds
And let ourselves mend

From the thoughts and feelings
That hold us back
How can we overcome
Our sense of lack

So that we can discover
Our purpose in life
Let go of the pain
And end our strife

What will it take
For us to see
How we can serve
And be set free

From the mental prison
We create in our mind
To love ourselves
And be more kind

Anxiety can cripple you
Down to the bone
It's not easy
Walking your path alone

When life becomes
Too much to bear
Bring your palms together
Bow in prayer

God will catch
The tears that fall
Know that He is with you
As you give it your all

Helping you through
The darkest night
So that you can witness
The beauty of the light

To see the smile
Cracking on your face
Bow your head
Surrender with grace

He will teach you
To become whole
So that you can share your gift
The light in your soul

SPRING SHOWERS

When we listen
To gentle spring showers
We get lost in the rhythm
For hours and hours

Giving ourselves
The rest that we need
Life doesn't have to move
At blinding speed

It's OK
To take a break
Find peace inside
For goodness sake

This world forces us
To go, go, go
We never get the chance
To get lost in the flow

Allowing our minds
To wander in bed
We race through life
Like the living dead

Trying so hard
To be something we're not
Know that this life
Is all that you've got

So take the time
To appreciate yourself
By going within
You discover your wealth

Allowing you
To release the past
As the world whirls around you
Going nowhere fast

We are so accustomed
To doing what we're told
To live our lives in misery
As we begin to grow old

When will we learn
To change our ways
Get lost in the magic
And step out of the haze

This life that you have
Is a beautiful gift
You need to take the time
And let your perspective shift

So that you can follow
The voice inside
Listen to your heart
Let it be your guide

GURUJI

The dispeller of darkness
The bringer of light
Trust in the divine
And you will shine bright

The path of the guru
Is no easy feat
Bow your head
And find your seat

Prayer will teach you
How to let go
Creating the space inside
To learn and grow

It is only by walking
Through the dark of the night
That we come to appreciate
The beauty of the light

Bathing us
In our true form
So that we can go within
And learn to transform

The limiting views
Holdings us back
So we can move forward
And get back on track

To fulfill our potential
Our mission on Earth
Requires us to face our fears
And discover our worth

To know the truth
Eternal and free
When you understand energy
You will understand me

You are not limited
By time and space
Energy is infinite
It's time that we face

The misunderstandings
That we all hold
About the truth of the Self
It's time to be bold

Step forward with courage
And rise with love
Dispel the darkness
With the light from above

Bringing this world
Into the Fifth Dimension
Through the guru's grace
We find Ascension

HIDDEN CURRENTS

How can I feel
Complete within myself
To know the truth of my being
Is the greatest wealth

It is so easy
To be led astray
When we look to others
To guide the way

The voice of truth
Lies inside
Listen to your heart
And allow it to guide

It will help you
Stay the course
Let go of control
There is no need to force

The current will take you
Where you need to be
So you can let go of the pain
And set yourself free

From the expectations
That society holds
Based on cultural values
And the things we've been told

It is time
To release the past
To create a new future
Find peace at last

Learn to trust
The voice inside
And face your fears
With nothing to hide

It is only by being
Authentic and real
That you give others permission
To truly feel

So that they can let go
And learn to shine bright
We rise like the stars
And illuminate the night

WORLD OF THE ANCIENTS

This is the world that lies
In the subconscious realm
A desolate void
Where God takes the helm

Aligning you
With what you know is true
So that light can shine
In all that you do

You were created
From the Cosmic Source
Allow your life to unfold
And take its course

You came to this planet
With a mission to fulfill
It is time to rise
Stop standing so still

We need you now
To shine the light
Awaken the others
Help them dissolve the night

So they can rise
To their highest potential
Share your gifts
Your part is essential

To change the consciousness
That exists on the Earth
Some ideas need to die
So that others can find birth

Like the rise of Unity
Oneness and truth
So that a future exists
For the kids and our youth

There is no sense in destroying
All that we need
Why are we consumed
With senseless greed

What does it take
To feel fulfilled
You will find inner peace
When your mind is stilled

This is the world
That the ancients knew
Full of peace and bliss
And a love that was true

What will it take
For us to find
This beautiful space
And stop being so blind

To the divinity that lies
Within you now
Stop and listen
It will show you how

To discover the mysteries
Of this ancient world
Let go and surrender
As the serpent is unfurled

GUARDIAN ANGEL

What if you always had someone
Watching your back
Guiding you through
When you get off track

Keeping your best interests
Close at heart
So that you can serve
And play your part

Know that you
Will always be protected
Even when things don't go
Exactly as expected

For you are being watched over
By a guardian from above
Allow yourself to feel
Unconditional love

For that is the way
That I love you
In complete surrender
You will find what is true

GUARDIAN ANGEL

The force that sets
Celestial bodies in motion
Is the same that is found
Through love and devotion

This is the surest sign
Of one that is pure
The power of love
Will make you strong and sure

That the spiritual path
Is the right one for you
Discover your Self
And find what is true

The eternal mystery
That lies inside
Has secrets to reveal
When you let go of your pride

Surrender the construct
Of your personality
And you wlll be shown
A new reality

One the exists
In love and light
An infinite expanse
A sea of white

There you will be shown
The truth of your form
The peaceful centre
The eye of the storm

Where you will witness
The beginning and the end
By understanding this
You begin to transcend

Beyond the confines
Of the senses and mind
Where the wheel of karma
Can no longer bind

Letting you live
Eternal and free
By liberating others
And helping them see

GUARDIAN ANGEL

How they can step forward
And learn to shine
When you know the truth
You will know the divine

As a guardian angel
Protecting the Earth
It is up to you
To show others their worth

So that we can rise
And learn to stand tall
On the path to fulfillment
You must give it your all

Trust your intuition
To guide you through
So that love can radiate
In all that you do

You are a messenger
A beacon of light
Spread your wings
It's time to take flight

And lift this world
Into the dimensions above
Where humanity will learn
Unconditional love

This is the root
Of all spiritual tradition
Embody love
And fulfill your mission

SERVE THYSELF

KARMA: THE YOGA OF ACTION

The final path outlined in the Bhagavad Gita is the path of karma yoga, the yoga of action. This path is the most beneficial for those who are action takers, doers, and people who love to be busy.

A karma yogi's work is considered to be a form of prayer. Work is done in order to serve the divine as well as other beings on the planet.

Karma yoga is based on taking right action. Right action is action that is aligned with the yogi's life path and dharma. By following our path and purpose in life it allows us to become our authentic selves and do the highest work we can in service to others.

It is only through action
That we can change our course
And discover the light
Of the Eternal Source

In karma yoga we pursue our life's work for the virtue of the work alone. We release our attachment to the fruits of our labours and offer our work as a form of prayer in selfless service towards the divine. In this way we learn the value of love and giving.

By synthesizing all the paths of yoga outlined in the Gita a yogi is able to move towards spiritual freedom faster and easier. These three paths allow the divine that lies within all to be seen, loved, and served.

Through the practice of yoga all of humanity can be liberated to the true light of the soul. If you want to follow the path of karma yoga you could ask yourself "How can I serve for the highest good of all?"

You came here to serve
For the highest good of all
Find your courage and strength
Stop playing so small

DIVINE LIGHT

What will it take
For humanity to see
The divine within all
And be set free

From the shackles of greed
Disillusion and fear
As we destroy the planet
Year after year

Feeling like we
Are never enough
Feeding our ego's
And buying more stuff

There is nothing wrong
With consuming to live
But when will we learn
To love and give

This is the power
That unites us all
It is time that we rise
And learn to stand tall

For this beautiful Earth
That we call our home
There is no reason for us
To feel so alone

As anxiety and depression
Continue to rise
And we constantly feed
On the media's lies

We do not understand
Why we feel so disconnected
Or how societies changes
Cause us to be affected

We have lost our connection
To the primordial source
The connection to Self
That sets our life's course

When we discover
The values we hold
We will no longer accept
The lies we've been told

By political leaders
And corporate execs
It's time for us
To stand and flex

The biggest muscle
That we have to share
The one in our heart
When we bow in prayer

With gratitude and love
For all beings on this Earth
It's time that we learn
To find our worth

Nothing is lacking
Inside of you
Connect to your essence
And find what is true

You will come to know
The light of the divine
The same way the stars
Rise and shine

DIVINE LIGHT

So that you can share
A different perspective
And help bring change
To the social collective

People feel powerless
Under the crushing weight
Of a society that is
Consumed in hate

Always trying
To get ahead
While holding on
By just a thread

The universe will always
Provide what you need
When you let go of fear
And senseless greed

So that you can share
The light from above
And show us the power
Of unconditional love

LAKSHMI

She is the goddess
Of abundance and wealth
We bow to her
And come to know our Self

Eternally free
Like the clouds in the sky
Rolling across the plains
Where the eagles fly

Soaking the soil
Awakening the seed
Always providing us
With what we need

To take that next step
To elevate our lives
To grow with courage
As our life force thrives

Know that you will always
Have her support
Even when it feels
Like you're coming up short

The challenges you face
Will help you grow
So that you can share with others
All that you know

The journey of the soul
Is for you to take
Know there will be times
That cause you to break

To question the life
That you have been living
In the search for truth
You must start giving

For it is in
The purity of heart
That you will create change
And then you can start

To build a new life
With what you want to see
It is up to you to give
And be all you can be

She will show you
That you are always enough
You are not defined
By the value of your stuff

Self worth is created
When you let yourself heal
From the wounds of the past
That caused you to reel

That broke your spirit
And consumed you with despair
Know that in your darkest moments
She will be there

To lift your head
When you feel weak
So that you can move through life
Even when it seems bleak

Be grateful for the moment
That you have right now
Find peace in the present
It will show you how

You can overcome
The emotions you feel
Let go of the past
Let yourself heal

It is through the power
Of the meditative force
That we can walk a new path
And chart a new course

That sees us reaping
The abundance of fall
By discovering your Self
You can have it all

QUANTUM LEAP

JUSTIN WESENBERG

What does it take
For us to take a leap
Jump forward in our lives
Wake up from our sleep

Operating on autopilot
From day to day
It's easy to see
How we've lost the way

To happiness and joy
To a life that is free
Sometimes your habits
Don't let you see

What's brainwashing you
And holding you back
Let go of the pain
Your sense of lack

Know that the universe
Will always provide
When you learn to give
And let go of your pride

You are here
To share your gifts
Help heal the planet
As the consciousness shifts

Aligning us
With love and light
To dissolve the darkness
So we can shine bright

Fulfilling our mission
Our purpose on Earth
Requires us to know
The value of our worth

Stop tearing yourself down
And building others up
Find love for yourself
And start filling your cup

It is from this space
That you will learn to serve
Bringing the abundance and grace
That you truly deserve

YOGANANDA

The yogi that travelled
From East to West
So we could go within
And do our best

To live a life
Of love and peace
When will the violence stop
When will the hatred cease

When we can see
All beings as One
We illuminate the planet
Like the glowing sun

No more suffering
No more pain
No one has to lose
So that you can gain

Life is not
A competitive race
When will you give up the madness
And stop the chase

Trying to find
Your next fix
And falling for all
The latest tricks

Distracting you
From your true form
Know that it is from the Light
That you are born

You are a cosmic creation
From the Universal Source
Understand this law
And you will no longer force

The way that you believe
The world should be
Set the example
So that others can see

Their unlimited nature
Their true Self
Know that in Spirit
You find infinite wealth

This is what
The highest yogi's teach
In order to manifest
You must watch your speech

Let your words
Bless our ears
So that we can dissolve
Our greatest fears

About how we
Are never enough
Filling the void
By buying more stuff

Constantly consuming
With no end in sight
Terrified to face
The Eternal Night

Know that death
Cannot destroy the soul
You will be given another chance
To fulfill your role

But while you're here
Why not do your best
So when your body lays down
Your soul can rest

THE LIGHT

Who ever told you
That you are not enough
Where do you go to hide
When life gets rough

Is it in the bottle
Or in the fridge
Or on a mountaintop
Climbing a ridge

We push the feelings down
We try to forget
We spend our whole lives
Living in regret

Feeling like we
Are not worthy of love
Not seeing the light
Sent from above

Purifying us
With it's holy flame
Dissolving us
From this worldly game

THE LIGHT

So that we can serve
With love in our eyes
And let go of the past
As a part of us dies

No longer blinded
By the illusions of the world
You will find the truth
As the serpent is unfurled

Rising up
From the base of the spine
To the crown lotus
Causing you to shine

Brighter than the stars
That illuminate the night
You came to the planet
So that you could shine bright

To light the path
So that others can grow
You must share the truth
And all that you know

When you come to know God
Who lies within
You will absolve yourself
Of all you believe is sin

You will see yourself
Holy and pure
This will make you
Strong and sure

That the spirit of God
Lives in all things
When you see this light
You can spread your wings

And become a messenger
An angel of the Earth
Through unconditional love
You show others their worth

Leading us
To a new reality
That sees the dissolution
Of all this brutality

THE LIGHT

So that all beings can live
Eternal and free
When you come to know truth
Then you will truly see

The beauty that lies
In all of creation
So that you can evolve
And raise your vibration

And learn to move
With the holy source
It will allow spirit
To change your course

Living your life
Aligned with the heart
Sometimes requires
A brand new start

Don't be afraid
To shed the past
It's time to find
Peace at last

Know that you
Are always protected
When all you see
Is the light reflected

You will learn to feel
Whole and complete
When you bow in surrender
In a meditative seat

This will teach you
True humility
So that you can find
Inner tranquility

Surrender to God
Let go of control
In the light you'll witness
The truth of the soul

OMNIPOTENT

Now is the time
To create the new
Let love come forth
In all that you do

Help them throw off
The burdens they bear
Let them dissolve in surrender
They're in divine care

You have much to learn
About the quantum field
This science will teach you
About the power you wield

As an omnipresent being
A maker of the divine
You were given this light
So that you could shine

Help awaken others
To the path of the soul
Help them find freedom
The highest goal

For them to dissolve
Into the cosmic flow
They must trust in God
And learn to let go

Of the personality construct
The thoughts of the mind
It is only through surrender
That you come to find

The essence of God
That lies within you
Stop trying to force
Let the light shine through

MOKSHA

What will it take
To set yourself free
Released from the expectations
Of what you should be

Learn to dive
Into the deep unknown
It is here that the cosmos
Come to be known

There are many people
All throughout history
That have dedicated their lives
To solving the Great Mystery

What does it mean
Where are we from
Why do we walk around
Feeling so glum

How can we learn
To change our view
So that we can discover
All that is true

The lovely parts
The bits we hide
It's time we learn
To let go of our pride

To bow with grace
To serve with love
Through these acts we embody
The light from above

Showing others
Through the beauty in your eyes
How love can transform
As your ego dies

Releasing you
From the body you bear
Trust in the light
You're in divine care

As you're birthed
Into the next dimension
Let yourself relax
Let go of the tension

It is through witnessing
The Primordial form
That your life will change
And completely transform

Awakening the energy
Of the Kundalini snake
Clearing you
Of all that is fake

So that you can know
The truth of the soul
In the light you will realize
That you are whole

Bow down in surrender
And you will see
The love will rise
And set you free

INNER EYE

When you learn to open
The inner eye
You will see untold realms
As you journey high

Into the infinite space
Of the Cosmic Self
It is here that we find
Untold wealth

As we connect
To the Universal Source
It allows us to chart
A new course

One that sees us
Guided by the heart
So that we can create
A brand new start

To step forward and start
Something new in our lives
We let go of the past
As the bird song cries

Ringing out
Through this sacred land
It is time we rise
And take a stand

Against the raging torrent
Of the mind
It's time that we stop
Being so blind

To the way that our actions
Affect the Earth
It's time that we learn
To find our worth

And teach others
Through the power of love
How they can embody
The light from above

To illuminate
Our beautiful home
And make sure that none of us
Have to walk alone

Embrace the journey
That lies ahead
Know that fear
Is all in your head

Holding you back
From your true potential
We need you now
Your gifts are essential

To help create
A brand new Earth
As the old paradigm dies
And another gives birth

From here we move
Into the Fifth Dimension
And align the planet
With the gates of Ascension

WHITE CRYSTAL WIZARD

We are all born
With the power to create
How you use this gift
Will shape your fate

We manifest our lives
Through thought, word, and deed
When we choose love
We are given all we need

To live our best lives
To share our gifts
It's up to us to change
As our consciousness shifts

Aligning us
With the power of the light
We are the wizards
Robed in white

Here to step forward
And awaken the Earth
To teach humanity
About what life is worth

WHITE CRYSTAL WIZARD

Like the river that flows
Open and pure
Put your faith in the divine
You will be strong and sure

That the path you are on
Is right for you
Ask to be shown the way
And you will find what is true

The light of the divine
Permeates through us all
It's time to rise
And stop playing so small

You came to the Earth
With a mission to fulfill
You must take action
And use your will

To create the change
That you wish to see
You must change first
Show others how to be

JUSTIN WESENBERG

A beacon of love
A being of light
You are here to show them
How they can shine bright

By casting off the shackles
Of the material world
The serpent will rise
As the mystery is unfurled

Opening the lotuses
As it rises through the body
You will know the truth
When you clear Sushumna Nadi

This will help you
To realize the Self
When you discover this
You'll find infinite wealth

And come to know
The Universal Form
That defies all logic
And worldly norms

So that you can share
Your divine gifts
Help awaken the planet
As the global consciousness shifts

GANESHA

The remover of obstacles
Guiding the way
To the beauty of a new dawn
A brand new day

Bringing abundance
Success and love
Embodying the divine
With wisdom from above

He will teach us
To be loving and kind
By controlling our thoughts
And controlling our mind

Meditate on him
And you will come to see
Your infinite self
Eternal and free

This is the abundance
Of the Eternal Self
Discover this within
And you will know real wealth

GANESHA

Is not just defined
By the money in the bank
What would we value
If the economy tanked

Love is the truth
Our cosmic connection
Understand this link
And show your affection

For the people in your life
That you hold dear
Rejoice with them
And hold them near

Relationships reflect
What you need to know
So that you can go within
And let yourself grow

To share your love
And what you hold true
So the light can shine
In all that you do

Whenever you are starting
Something new
Call on Ganesha
To guide you through

With a light that illuminates
Infinite space
Trust in him
And step forward with grace

OSIRIS

What does it take
For us to clearly see
The patterns that hold us back
And stop us from being free

You were told
As an early child
To stop your tantrums
Stop being so wild

Constrained and conditioned
By events beyond your control
And desperately trying
To make yourself feel whole

Life isn't always
An easy road
Sometimes it pays to stop
And put down the load

So that you can take out
Those bricks in your bag
The big heavy ones
That cause your spirits to sag

Learn to be light
Like the breeze in the trees
And you will find
Life moves with ease

You must trust
You will be shown the way
The same way that night
Follows the day

Step into the darkness
Embrace your shadow side
Have no fear
There is nothing to hide

For it has been written
In the Hall Of The Dead
The story of your life
Is all in your head

You can choose
To create powerful change
Set the power of your intention
And begin to rearrange

The quantum field
That lies all around
You can change your harmonics
Through the resonance of sound

To vibrate out
A golden glow
Solfeggio frequencies
Will help you to know

The power that lies
Within you now
That will change your fate
And show you how

You can create
And manifest your desires
Instead of feeling stuck
In the depths of the mires

Osiris is
The God of the Dead
Let go of your conditioning
It's all in your head

Then you will know
The eternity of the soul
Dissolve your fear
Learn to be whole

ABOUT THE AUTHOR

Justin Wesenberg is a reiki energy healer, author, yogi, and lightworker living in the beautiful Rocky Mountains of Canada.

His mission is to help all beings realize the divine light that lies within so that we can bring about unity consciousness on Earth.

To learn more visit: **justinwesenberg.com**

THE INVITATION

I'm offering you an invitation...

These invitations don't happen often, but I've got something special just for you!

I am going to teach you the **ONE** skill that will change your life more than any other skill you could learn...

It will help you find greater freedom, love, purpose, and peace...

If you want to discover what this one secret skill is and how it can change your life forever visit:

justinwesenberg.com/the-invitation

I'm looking forward to seeing you there!